COULD A CROCODILE PLAY BASKETBALL?

PLAY BASKETBALL?

...and other questions

Aleksei Bitskoff &
Camilla de la Bédoyère

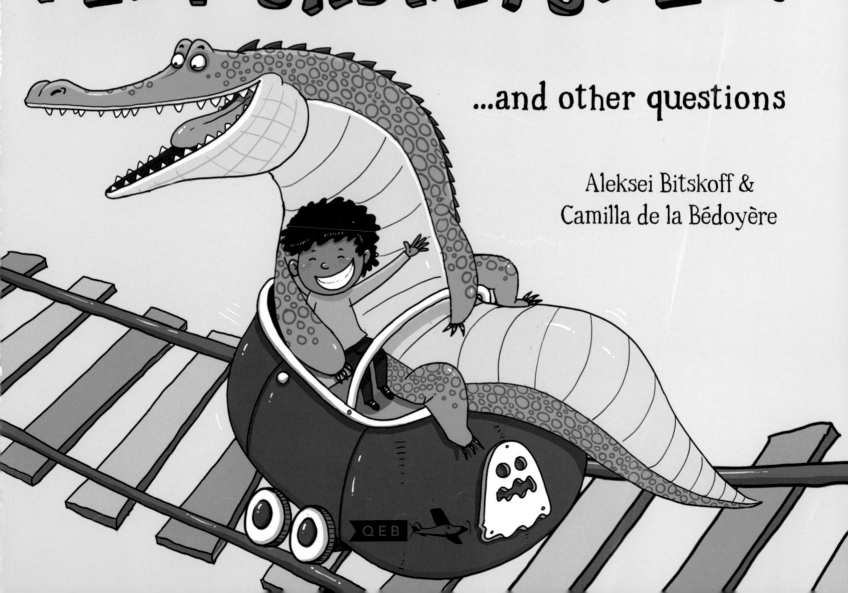

Saltwater crocodiles are the largest crocodiles in

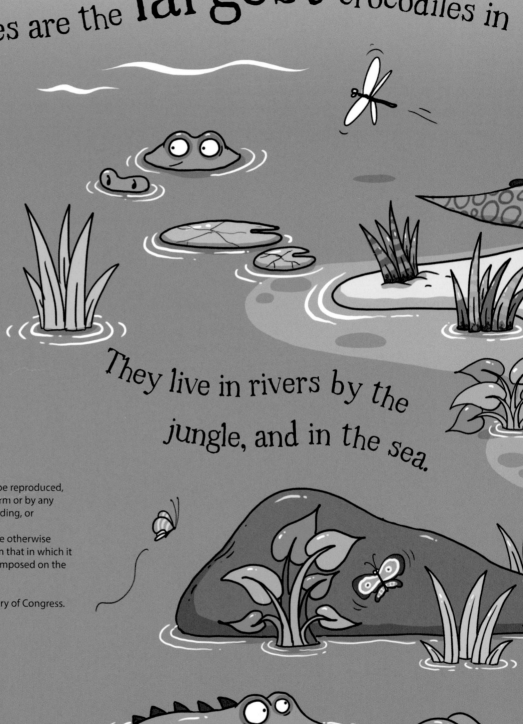

They live in rivers by the jungle, and in the sea.

Design: Duck Egg Blue
Editor: Carly Madden
Editorial Director: Victoria Garrard
Art Director: Laura Roberts-Jensen
Publisher: Maxime Boucknooghe

Copyright © QEB Publishing 2016

First published in the United States in 2016 by
Part of the Quarto Group
QEB Publishing
6 Orchard
Lake Forest
CA 92630

www.qed-publishing.co.uk

A CIP record for this book is available from the Library of Congress.

ISBN 978 1 60992 939 8

Printed in China

the world. They have HUGE jaws and lots of teeth.

Imagine if a crocodile came to stay.
What would he do?

What if a crocodile went to the carnival?

He would have fun riding on a **SPOOKY** ghost train, but he wouldn't be very **frightened.**

There are few animals in the jungle that are brave enough to fight a crocodile...

...he's too big and scary'.

Would a crocodile enjoy a snowball fight?

No! He would be a **cross croc.**

Crocodiles are reptiles, and reptiles cannot move when they are very cold.

Chilly crocs have to snooze until the sun comes out and warms them up.

But a cold croc might make a good...

...snow-croc!

Could a crocodile play basketball?

Yes, he could shoot a ball

**through
the
hoop,**

no problem!

The biggest crocodiles are
20 feet long.

They can run, stand on their back feet, and even leap into the air!

Crocodiles can run faster than most people.

What if a crocodile was very hungry?

He might begin his meal with a mouthful of stones!

Crocodiles swallow stones to help **grind up** the food in their stomachs.

Then he would start on a **giant plate** of food.

He could eat 1,100 pounds in one sitting. That's about

5,000

ham sandwiches!

Would a crocodile like to play with stuffed animals?

He might have **huge**, powerful jaws, but a crocodile could be gentle with stuffed animals.

Crocodiles don't have strollers for their babies, so in the jungle they carry their babies down to the river in their...

...enormous mouths!

Some crocodile dads watch over their babies to keep them safe.

What if a crocodile visited a castle?

He could swim in the moat.

Or he might pretend to be a knight...

His skin is almost as strong as a suit of armor because it is **covered in scales.**

The large scales on a crocodile's back have plates of bone inside them. Even another crocodile has trouble biting through them!

What would a crocodile like to do for fun?

He would enjoy a game of mini golf, but he wouldn't need a golf club. He could...

...WHACK the ball...

...with his mighty tail instead.

Crocodiles need strong tails because they use them for swimming in rivers, especially when they are chasing fish.

They also use their tail as a handy weapon!

What would a crocodile do if he lost a tooth?

He could leave one of his **BIG, shiny teeth** for the tooth fairy!

actual size!

Crocodiles have about 66 teeth, but if one tooth falls out a new one **grows** to replace it!

A crocodile grows about 3,000 teeth in its lifetime—that's about 60 times more teeth than you will ever have.

That's a lot of money from the tooth fairy!

Would a crocodile enjoy a sleepover?

Crocodiles don't like to sleep in beds.
They prefer to sleep in water.

He would have to find a watery place that's big enough
for him to **stretch out**.

Everyone would need to **tiptoe** around him, as crocodiles have incredible hearing—even underwater.

It's not a good idea to disturb a **sleeping crocodile!**

More about saltwater crocodiles

Crocodile is pointing to the places where he lives.
Can you see where you live?

FACT FILE

There are 13 types of crocodile and two types of alligator.

There were crocodile-like animals living alongside the dinosaurs, millions of years ago.

Saltwater crocodiles lay up to 90 eggs in a huge nest near the riverbank.

Male crocodiles can grow twice as big as females.

Crocodiles can live a long time. They may live to be as old as 100!

Saltwater crocodiles are the largest reptiles in the world.

Areas where saltwater crocodiles live

NORTH AMERICA

PACIFIC OCEAN

SOUTH AMERICA

Greetings from Australia!

POST CARD

I'm on my way home now and can't wait to dive into the lovely lagoon and go fishing. Thank you for looking after me!

I had lots of fun at the fair but my favorite vacation treat was mini golf. I can't wait to teach my crocodile friends how to play!

Love,
Crocodile X

SENT BY SALTWATER CROCODILE POST
NORTHERN TERRITORY, AUSTRALIA

1ST

Mr and Mrs Snap
118 Spiky Lane
Poole, CO 12345

1704092201122528877